STARTING
COOKING

Gill Harvey

Cookery specialist: Julia Kirby-Jones

Edited by Fiona Watt

**Designed by Sarah Bealham
and Maria Wheatley**

Illustrated by Norman Young

Photography by Amanda Heywood

Food stylist: Carole Handslip
Additional photography by Howard Allman
Series editor: Cheryl Evans

Contents

Before you begin

This book shows you how to start cooking using burners, a broiler and an oven. It explains many of the skills that will help you to cook and gives lots of tasty recipes for you to try.

A recipe tells you how to make something to eat. It has a list of the food you will need, called the ingredients. It also tells you which things to use. These are called kitchen utensils. Here you can see most of the utensils you will use in this book.

Staying clean

Roll up your sleeves. Wash your hands and put on an apron.

Always use clean utensils and wash everything up afterwards.

Wipe surfaces clean with a damp cloth. Wipe up anything that you spill on the floor straight away.

Rolling pin

Grater

Mixing bowl

Strainer

Saucepan

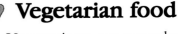

Vegetarian food

Vegetarians are people who don't eat meat or fish. Recipes with this picture next to them can be eaten by vegetarians.

Colander

Citrus juicer

Chopping board

Deep bowl

Keeping safe

Before you start, make sure there is an adult nearby to help you. Never leave the kitchen when burners or the broiler are on, and don't try to carry hot things that are too heavy for you.

Metal spatula

Rounded knife

Kitchen knives

Can opener

Ask an adult for help when you see this picture. Always ask for help when you turn on an electric stove, or if you need to light a gas stove.

Be extra careful when you see this picture. For example, be very careful when using sharp knives. Turn saucepan handles so they don't stick out.

This picture warns you that something is very hot. When you touch anything hot, wear oven mitts to protect you. Put hot things onto a heat-proof mat.

Remember to turn off the stove or the oven when you have finished with them. This picture reminds you when to turn something off.

Getting ready

Before you start cooking, read the recipe all the way through. Each one is enough for four people unless it says something else. Check that you have all the ingredients and utensils.

When you see a cooking skill written in **bold**, look at the bottom of the page. There you can find out where it is first explained. You can also find out more about cooking skills if you look on page 32.

Cake pans

Whisk

Oven mitts

Pastry brush

Vegetable peeler

Spatula

Wooden spoon

Cookie sheet

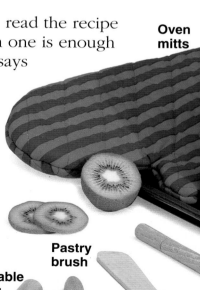

3

Getting started

When you cook, you measure things like flour and sugar using measuring cups. Make sure your ingredients are level with the top of the cup.

Sometimes, things are measured by weight, depending on how they are sold. Your recipe will tell you which way to measure.

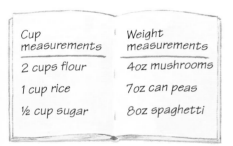

Cup measurements	Weight measurements
2 cups flour	4oz mushrooms
1 cup rice	7oz can peas
½ cup sugar	8oz spaghetti

A pinch is a very small amount of something like salt or pepper. It is what you can pick up between your finger and thumb.

You use a liquid measuring cup for things like milk and fruit juice. Pour them in slowly until they reach the right mark on the cup.

Put the cup onto a flat surface.

Tablespoons and teaspoons and are used to measure small amounts. Tablespoon is written "tbs" and teaspoon is written "tsp".

A level spoon

A rounded spoon

A heaped spoon

Crunchy muesli

You will need:
dried apricot pieces
banana chips
wheat flakes
oats
sunflower seeds
walnut pieces
raisins
milk
honey

cups, big bowl, tablespoon, measuring cup, teaspoon

You could put fresh fruit into the muesli, such as peaches or strawberries. Add them just before you eat it.

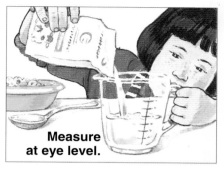

Measure at eye level.

Measure ¼ cup oats and put them into a big bowl. Add ¼ cup wheat flakes, ¼ cup banana chips and ¼ cup apricot pieces.

Add 2 rounded tbs raisins, 1 rounded tbs sunflower seeds and 3 rounded tbs walnuts. Mix everything together well.

Put into four dishes. Measure ½ cup of milk for each dish. Pour it over. Add 1 tsp of honey to each dish if you like sweet muesli.

Parts of a stove

The two main types of stoves are electric stoves and gas stoves. They usually have four burners, a broiler and an oven.

A broiler and its control knob may be above or below the rings or burners. If your broiler is hard to reach, ask an adult to help.

Here are oven knobs set at different temperatures. Convection ovens are not the same, so if you have one, read your instruction book.

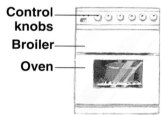

Control knobs
Broiler
Oven

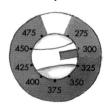

This oven is set at 300°F. This is a low heat for cooking things very slowly.

Each ring or burner has its own knob to control the heat. You can make each one hotter or cooler by turning the knob.

Recipes in this book give temperatures in °F for oven baking. They also tell you which shelf you should cook your food on.

Gas burners   **Electric rings**

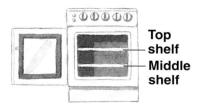

Top shelf
Middle shelf

This oven is set at medium heat. This can be between 325°F and 375°F.

This oven is set at 450°F. This is a hot oven, for cooking things like bread.

Using a broiler

A broiler cooks things very quickly on one side. To cook them on the other side, you have to turn them over. This can be tricky because the broiler and the food you are broiling become very hot, so ask an adult to help.

Cheese and ham toasties

For one toastie you will need:
2 slices white or brown bread
butter or margarine
1 slice cooked ham
2oz or ⅛ cup cheese
a tomato
some cucumber

grater
small plate
rounded knife
oven mitts
tongs
kitchen knife
chopping board

You can make vegetarian toasties by leaving out the ham. You could add tomato instead.

To make a cheese and tomato toastie, put some slices of tomato on top of the grated cheese before broiling it.

Grating

Put the grater on a plate. Hold it tightly with the holes you want to use facing away from you.

Hold the piece of food firmly and push it down the holes on the grater. Do this lots of times.

Stop grating when your fingers get close to the grater. A small piece of food will be left over.

Use a rounded knife.

Grate the cheese onto a plate. Turn the broiler to full heat. Spread butter on the slices of bread.

Turn one slice over so the butter is underneath. Put the slice of ham onto it. Sprinkle the cheese on top.

Chopping and slicing

To chop a tomato, hold it firmly, making a bridge with your fingers. Cut it in half. Put the halves down flat. Chop them in half again. Keep chopping until the pieces are the size you want them.

Lay the second slice of bread on top of the ham and cheese. The butter should be on the outside.

Place the toastie on the broiler rack. Slide the pan under the broiler. Watch it carefully until it turns brown.

To slice a tomato, cut down one side. Keep your fingers well away from the knife.

Try to cut thin slices.

To slice a cucumber, hold it firmly at one end. Cut thin slices from the other end.

Use tongs

Pull the broiler pan out. Turn the toastie over carefully, then broil it on the other side until it turns brown.

Cut the toastie into triangles. Cut slices of cucumber and tomato. Arrange them on a plate around the toastie.

Using an oven

Most ovens need time to heat up, so you need to turn them on before you start cooking. To do this, turn the oven knob to the temperature given in the recipe. Usually, this makes a light come on which goes out when the oven is hot enough. Remember that if you have a fan oven it may be different, so check in your instruction book.

Baked potatoes

For two potatoes you will need:
2 large baking potatoes
cooking oil
butter or margarine

For the fillings, choose:
6⅛oz can tuna
1 tbs mayonnaise
7oz can sweet corn
or:
¼ cup cheese
British-style pickle

stiff brush for cleaning potatoes, fork, paper towels, cookie sheet, oven mitts, kitchen knife, can opener, tablespoon, small bowl, grater, plate, teaspoon

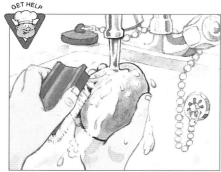

Turn the oven on to 400°F. Scrub the potatoes with the brush in cold water to remove any dirt.

Use the top shelf.

Put the tray of potatoes into the oven. Cook them for about one hour, then take them out carefully.

If they are still hard, cook them for another 30 minutes and test them again. If they are soft, cut them in half.

Prick the potatoes all over with a fork. Wipe on some oil with paper towels. Put them onto a cookie sheet.

Test the potatoes with a kitchen knife. If they are cooked, they will feel soft all the way through.

Put a little butter or margarine into each potato. Put the filling you have chosen on top (see right).

Try a filling of soured cream and chopped chives.

Using a microwave

GET HELP

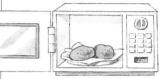

Microwaves cook food more quickly than other ovens.

Never put anything metal in a microwave.

To cook potatoes, prick them with a fork. Put them into the microwave on paper towels. You will need to look in your instruction book to find out how long to cook them for.

Tuna, mayonnaise and sweet corn filling

GET HELP

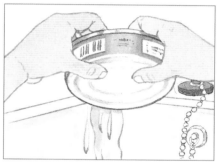

Pile the filling onto the potato.

Open the cans of tuna and sweet corn. You may need an adult to help.

Drain the liquid from the cans by holding down the lid and tipping it into the sink.

Put the tuna into a small bowl. Mix in the mayonnaise and 2 tbs sweet corn.

Tuna, mayonnaise and sweet corn filling, and cheese filling

Cheese and pickle filling

Grate the cheese onto a plate. Put half on each potato. Add some British-style pickle with a teaspoon.

Baking cakes

When you bake a cake, you may be tempted to open the oven door halfway through cooking to check it. This can make the cake sink in the middle, so wait until it is almost cooked before you have a look.

Brownies

You will need:
½ cup margarine, ½ cup packed brown sugar, ½ cup granulated sugar, 2 eggs, ½ cup chopped walnuts, ½ cup self-rising flour, ½ cup baking cocoa, 1 tsp vanilla, 1 level tsp baking powder

small square or oblong pan (about 9 x 9in), scissors, greaseproof paper, paper towels, wooden spoon, mixing bowl, small bowl, fork, sifter, metal spoon, oven mitt, kitchen knife, wire rack

Mixing bowl

Turn the oven to 350°F. Grease or line the pan. Cream the margarine and sugar together.

Crack the eggs by tapping them sharply on the edge of a bowl. Carefully break them in half into the bowl.

Greasing and lining cake pans

To grease a pan, either spray it with cooking oil spray, or wipe the inside of the pan with a paper towel dipped in margarine.

To line a cake pan, draw around it on greaseproof paper. Draw another square around it, big enough to cover the sides of the pan.

Cut out the big square. Cut from the edge to the four corners of the small square. Fold up the edges. Fit the paper into the pan.

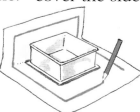

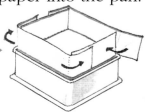

Mix the yolks and whites with a fork. Add slowly to the sugar and margarine, beating all the time.

Mix in the walnuts. Spoon the flour, cocoa and baking powder into a sifter. Shake into the mixture. Fold in.

Beating, folding and creaming

Beating means mixing firmly with a wooden spoon or an electric mixer. Ask an adult to help with a mixer.

GET HELP

Use the middle shelf.

Spoon the mixture into the pan. Smooth the top with the spoon. Cook for 40 minutes, then take it out.

Cook for five more minutes if not cooked.

TURN IT OFF

Press the top of the cake lightly. It will spring back into shape when you lift your finger if it is cooked.

Creaming is beating margarine or butter and sugar together so that they become a smooth mixture.

To fold in, you mix gently with a metal spoon or flat knife. Try to burst as few bubbles of air as possible.

You could sprinkle powdered sugar over the squares.

BE CAREFUL

Allow to cool for ten minutes, then cut the cake into squares with a kitchen knife. Put onto a wire rack.

Cut and turn slowly.

Meaty oven dishes

When you cook meat in an oven you can add lots of things to it like herbs and vegetables, which make it really tasty. This is because the meat takes a long time to cook, so the different flavors have plenty of time to get into it. The taste of the meat makes the vegetables delicious, too.

You can find out how to cook rice to eat with your chicken on pages 20-21.

Cooking chicken

Always wash chicken before you cook it. If it is frozen, make sure it is thawed completely. Always wash your hands after touching raw chicken, and check that it is properly cooked before you eat it.

Chicken parcels

You will need:
4 chicken quarters
4oz mushrooms
1 small red pepper
1 small green pepper
1 small onion
¼ cup margarine
   or butter
1 lemon
salt

paper towels, kitchen knife, chopping board, kitchen foil, scissors, citrus juicer, cookie sheet, oven mitts

GET HELP

Turn the oven to 400°F. Wash the chicken quarters under the cold tap. Pat them dry with paper towels.

BE CAREFUL

Wash and chop the mushrooms. Wash the peppers and slice them up. Peel the onion and chop it into thin strips.

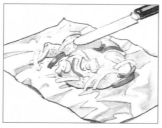

Push down and twist.

Cut four squares of foil, each big enough to wrap around a piece of chicken. Put a piece in the middle of each one.

Divide the vegetables between the pieces, then wash your hands. Dab on some margarine or butter. Add a pinch of salt.

Cut the lemon in half with a kitchen knife. Squeeze the juice from one half and sprinkle it over the chicken.

Fold the foil around the pieces, folding over twice on top, then twice at each end. Put the parcels on a cookie sheet.

More chopping and slicing

To chop an onion, hold it firmly. Cut off both ends, then peel off all the brown skin.

Put the onion on one end. Hold it making a bridge with your fingers. Chop it in half.

Put the flat sides down and cut across in strips. You can then cut each strip into little pieces.

Use the top shelf.

Cook for one hour. Take the tray out and open the foil, being careful of the steam. Cook uncovered for 10-15 minutes.

To chop a pepper, hold it at the thinner end and slice off the end with the stalk.

Take out the rest of the stalk and the core. Scrape the seeds from inside the pepper.

Slice the pepper into rounds or strips. You can then chop them into smaller pieces if you want.

Test by sticking a kitchen knife into the meat. If it is cooked, the meat will be white all the way to the bone.

13

Using the stove top

Burners can get very, very hot. This means you need to watch carefully as you cook to make sure the food doesn't boil over the edge of the pan. You can stop things from sticking to the bottom of the pan by stirring with a wooden spoon.

Summer dessert

You will need:
1½lb fresh or frozen mixed soft fruit (such as raspberries, blackberries, strawberries or blueberries)
½ cup sugar
2 tbs water
10-12 slices white bread

colander, medium saucepan, wooden spoon, chopping board, kitchen knife, deep bowl, cup, small plate, weight such as cans, large plate

Put all the fruit into a colander. Wash it under a tap. Pull off all the leaves and stalks with your fingers.

Boiling and simmering

HOT

To bring something to a boil, turn the burner to full heat. When the food bubbles a lot, it is boiling.

To simmer something bring it to a boil, then turn the heat down until the food is bubbling just a little bit.

HOT

Put the fruit, water and sugar into a saucepan. Place the saucepan on a burner. Bring the mixture to a boil.

Make the slices overlap.

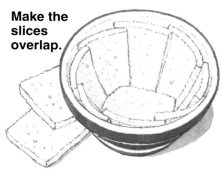

Cut the crusts off the slices of bread. Line the bowl with the slices. Save two or three of them for the top.

HOT **Try not to break up the fruit.**

TURN IT

Turn down the heat and simmer the mixture for five minutes. Stir very gently with a wooden spoon.

Spoon the fruit into the bowl. Save half a cup of fruit for later. Put the rest of the bread on top.

You could try summer dessert with cream.

Winter dessert

Winter dessert is made in exactly the same way as summer dessert, but with different fruit.

You will need:
11oz can mandarin oranges
14oz can cherry pie filling
⅓ cup sugar
¼ cup apple juice
¼ cup water
10-12 slices bread

Open the cans of oranges and cherry pie filling. Empty them into a saucepan with all the other ingredients except for the bread. Simmer the mixture for five minutes, stirring gently. Line the bowl with bread, then use the mixture in the same way as the fruit in the summer dessert.

Fit a small plate over the dessert. Put weights such as cans on top. Leave it to chill overnight in a refrigerator.

Take the plate and weight off the dessert. Put a large plate over it. Turn the plate and bowl upside down.

Shake the bowl and lift it off slowly, leaving the dessert on the plate. Pour the cup of fruit over it.

15

Pasta dishes

Pasta, like potatoes or rice, is a basic food. This means that you can use it in all sorts of different meals and add lots of tasty things to it. There are many kinds of pasta. This recipe uses spaghetti but you could try using other pasta shapes, like shells or twists.

Spaghetti bolognese

Chop the onion, pepper and mushrooms. Put the oil into a saucepan. Turn a ring or burner to medium heat.

Heat the oil. Add the onion, mushrooms and pepper and cook gently for four minutes until soft.

You will need:
1 onion
1 green pepper
4oz mushrooms
1 tbs cooking oil
8oz ground beef
14oz can tomatoes
14oz can tomato sauce
2 tsp Italian seasoning
1 rounded tbs tomato paste
salt and pepper
8oz spaghetti
some grated cheese

kitchen knife, chopping board, two large saucepans, wooden spoon, can opener, fork, colander, grater, plate

Add the minced beef. Stir it until it is all brown and none of it looks red. This is called browning.

Serve the spaghetti bolognese right away with grated cheese.

Open the cans of sauce and tomatoes. Stir into the pan with the tomato paste, seasoning, and a pinch of salt and pepper.

Vegetarian sauce

Make a vegetarian sauce by leaving out the ground beef. You could add more mushrooms, another green pepper, a red pepper or some black olives instead.

If the sauce begins to spit, turn the heat down further.

Bring to a **boil**, then turn the heat down low. **Simmer** for 30 minutes, stirring from time to time.

Cook the spaghetti in the other saucepan (see below). Drain, then serve it on plates with the sauce spooned on top.

The pasta test

If you cook pasta for too long it goes slimy and sticks together, so you need to test it as it cooks. Take some out with a fork. Let it cool, then taste it. It is cooked when just firm, not too soft but not crunchy.

Cooking pasta

Half-fill a large saucepan with water. Add a pinch of salt. Turn on a burner. Bring to a boil.

Place the pasta carefully in the water. If it is spaghetti, push it down gradually with a spoon as it softens.

Stir and bring to a boil again. Turn the heat down. Simmer for the time it says on the packet and test it.

Add 1 tbs oil to the pan to stop it from sticking.

Most pasta cooks in about ten minutes.

When cooked, ask an adult to help you drain the pasta by tipping it into a colander over the sink.

Cooking with eggs

Eggs can be cooked in lots of different ways. One of the special ways you can use them is to cook things that are very light to eat. You do this by whisking the egg white before you use it. This adds lots of air to it and makes it go white and frothy.

Lemon surprise pudding

You will need:

1 large lemon	2 tbs butter
2 eggs	½ cup milk
½ cup sugar	¼ cup self-rising flour

grater, small plate, kitchen knife, chopping board, citrus juicer, mixing bowl, saucer, egg cup, cup, small bowl, sifter, wooden spoon, whisk, metal spoon, medium oven-proof dish, oven mitts

GET HELP

Separating eggs

Crack the egg on the side of a cup. Break it open over a small saucer, being careful not to break the yolk.

Put an egg cup over the egg yolk. Tip the white into a small bowl. Lift off the egg cup and tip the yolk into a cup.

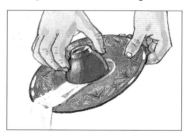

Try not to grate the white pith underneath the rind.

Heat the oven to 375°F. **Grate** half a teaspoon of rind from the lemon, using the fine holes.

Separate the eggs (see left). Put the egg white into a small bowl and put the yolks into the mixing bowl.

Cut the lemon in half and squeeze the juice from it. Put the juice into the mixing bowl with the rind.

The mixture is quite runny.

Sift the flour into the mixing bowl. Add the sugar and butter. **Beat** together well, then beat in the milk.

This dish is called a "surprise" because when you cut through the spongy top you find a yummy lemony sauce at the bottom.

Whisking egg whites

Recipes often ask you to whisk egg white until stiff. This means that when you lift the whisk it stands up in little triangles or peaks.

With a hand whisk, turn your wrist round and round quickly. It can take quite a long time for the white to go stiff.

To use an egg beater, hold it up straight and turn the handle. Ask an adult to help with an electric mixer.

Whisk the egg white until stiff (see right). **Fold** into the mixture. Pour the mixture into the oven-proof dish.

HOT

Use the middle shelf.

TURN IT OFF

Cook it for 35 minutes. If it is firm and golden brown, it is ready. If not, cook it for five more minutes.

Folding in - p.11

Cooking with rice

You can use rice as a main part of many different meals. For example, you could cook savory rice and eat it on its own, or boil some rice and cook something else to eat with it. Try it with chicken parcels (see pages 12-13).

Savory rice

You will need:
4oz mushrooms
1 red pepper
1 onion
14oz can tomatoes
2 tbs cooking oil
1¼ cup long grain white rice
7oz can peas or green beans
1 cup hot water
1 tbs soy sauce
pinch of salt
1 vegetable bouillon cube

kitchen knife
chopping board
can opener
tablespoon
large saucepan
wooden spoon
measuring cups

Wash the mushrooms and **chop** them into quarters. Chop the pepper and onion. Open the can of tomatoes.

Turn on a ring or burner to low heat and put the oil in a saucepan. Heat it very gently for a minute or two.

You could try eating your savory rice with chopsticks.

Add the onion. Stir and cook for four minutes. Add the mushrooms and red pepper. Cook for three more minutes.

Add the rice. Cook for two minutes, stirring all the time with a wooden spoon to stop it from sticking.

Add the can of tomatoes, peas or beans, water, soy sauce and salt. Crumble the bouillon cube into the mixture.

Boiling rice

1. Weigh out 2oz rice for each person. Half-fill a big saucepan with water and add a pinch of salt. Turn on a ring or burner.

2. Bring the water to a **boil.** Add the rice. Bring to a boil again, then simmer the rice for the time it says on the packet.

Most rice cooks in about 20-25 minutes.

3. After the right amount of time, take out a few grains of rice with a fork to test them. They should be firm, but not crunchy.

4. When the rice is cooked, ask an adult to help you drain it with a strainer over the sink. Shake all the water out of the strainer.

Let it cool slightly before you taste it.

Mix everything together. **Simmer** for 15-20 minutes, stirring gently from time to time to stop it from sticking.

Test the rice (see above). If it is not yet cooked and the rice is getting dry, add a little more water.

Find out more: Chopping - p.13 Boiling and simmering - p.14

Rubbing in and rolling out

Rubbing in is a skill you sometimes use to mix butter or margarine into flour. You often have to rub in when you make dough mixtures like pastry dough or scone dough. You can roll out most kinds of dough with a rolling pin.

Rubbing in

1. To rub in, cut the margarine or butter into pieces. Add it to the flour.

2. Mix and cut with a rounded knife until the butter is coated in flour.

3. Rub the mixture between your fingers, lifting it and letting it drop.

4. When the butter is mixed in well, the mixture looks like breadcrumbs.

Apple scones

You will need:
1 medium cooking apple
1½ cups self-rising flour
1 level tsp baking powder
6 tbs margarine
⅓ cup sugar
¼ cup milk
a little extra milk

cookie sheet, paper towels, chopping board, vegetable peeler, kitchen knife, mixing bowl, sifter, rounded knife, wooden spoon, rolling pin, spatula, pastry brush, oven mitts, wire rack

GET HELP

BE CAREFUL

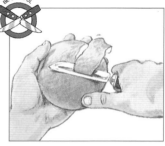

Heat the oven to 400°F. **Grease** the cookie sheet with some margarine or cooking oil spray.

Hold the apple firmly. Peel it with a vegetable peeler by scraping towards you with the sharp edge.

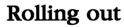

**Use a
small kitchen knife.**

Rolling out

Sprinkle flour over a clean, dry surface. Put the dough onto it. Rub flour over the rolling pin.

Hold the apple, making a bridge with your fingers. Cut it in half, then into quarters.

Hold each quarter firmly. Carefully cut the core from each one, then chop them all into little pieces.

Sift the flour and baking powder into a mixing bowl. Rub in the margarine. Stir in the sugar.

Press the dough down a little then roll gently and evenly. If the rolling pin sticks, add more flour.

Add the apple. Stir in the milk and make a ball of dough. It should be soft but not sticky.

Roll out the ball of dough (see right) until it is a round shape about 2½cm (1in) thick.

Cut the dough into eight pieces. Place them on the cookie sheet with a spatula. Brush with milk.

To make a round shape, roll a little, then stop. Turn the dough slightly and shape the edge. Roll again.

Apple scones are good as part of a picnic or packed lunch.

Bake for 20-25 minutes on the top shelf. They are ready when golden brown. Cool on a wire rack.

Find out more: Greasing cake pans - p.10   23

Making bread

When you make bread you use yeast, which makes the bread dough rise and the bread light to eat. The yeast also makes the dough become smooth and springy. This means that it is easy to make it into different shapes before you cook it. There are three shapes suggested here, but you could try making other ones.

Here you can see what cottage rolls and twists look like when they are cooked.

Bread rolls

For 8 rolls you will need :
½ cup warm water
1 level tsp dried yeast
1 level tsp sugar
1½ cups plain white flour (not self-rising flour)
½ level tsp salt
a little milk

tablespoon, small bowl, teaspoon, sifter, mixing bowl, wooden spoon, plastic foodwrap, cookie sheet, paper towels, kitchen knife, pastry brush, oven mitts

The water must be just warm, not hot.

Put 2 tbs of the warm water into a small bowl. Add the yeast and sugar and stir everything together well.

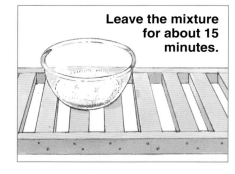

Leave the mixture for about 15 minutes.

Leave the bowl in a warm place, such as a kitchen cabinet, until the mixture becomes frothy on top.

Sift the flour and salt into a mixing bowl. Make a hole in the middle. Pour in the frothy yeast mixture.

Add the rest of the warm water. Mix with a wooden spoon until it all sticks together to make a dough.

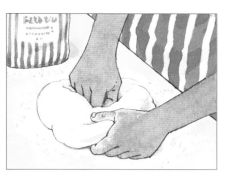

The dough will become about twice as big as it was before.

Make the dough into a ball with your hands. Knead it for ten minutes (see below). Put it back into the bowl.

Cover the bowl with plastic foodwrap and put it in a warm place. Leave it to rise for at least an hour.

Heat the oven to 425°F. **Grease** a cookie sheet. Knead the dough again for five minutes.

Put a little ball on top of a bigger one to make a cottage roll.

To make a twist, make a sausage then tie it in a knot.

Bake for five more minutes if not cooked.

Cut the dough into eight pieces. Make them into balls, or shape them into cottage rolls or twists, as above.

Put the rolls back in a warm place for 15 minutes to let them rise again, then brush them with a little milk.

Bake the rolls for about 15 minutes. They are cooked if they sound hollow when you tap them underneath.

Kneading

Sprinkle flour over a clean, dry surface. Stretch the dough out, pushing away from you.

Fold the dough over, then push it back into a ball. Stretch it out again. Keep stretching and folding it.

Stop when the dough is stretchy and you can make a ball that is round and smooth.

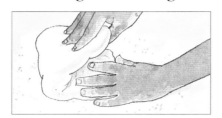

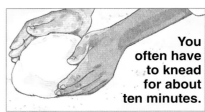

You often have to knead for about ten minutes.

A pizza meal

You can use bread dough to make the base for pizzas. This recipe gives some ideas for toppings, but you could try all kinds of tasty things like fresh tomato, onion, black olives or different kinds of pepper. Some of these toppings are on the pizza in the photograph. You could make a green salad to eat with your pizza.

Mini pizzas

For four pizzas you will need:

8oz bread dough
(see pages 24-25)
4 rounded tbs tomato paste
4 tbs water
½ tsp Italian seasoning
4oz cheese (1 cup grated)
2oz mushrooms
1 large slice cooked ham
1 green pepper

utensils for
making dough
(see page 24),
chopping board, kitchen knife,
small bowl, tablespoon, grater,
plate, two cookie sheets,
paper towels, wooden spoon,
colander, bowl for salad

**For a green
salad you
will need:**

a small head of lettuce
cucumber
two celery sticks

colander, large
bowl, kitchen knife,
chopping board

Follow the recipe for bread on pages 24-25, as far as leaving the dough for an hour in a warm place.

While the dough is rising, **slice** the ham, pepper and mushrooms. Mix the tomato paste, seasoning and water.

26

Find out more: Slicing - p.7, p.13

Grate the cheese carefully onto a plate. **Grease** the two cookie sheets and heat the oven to 425°F.

Don't worry if they are not quite round.

Put two balls of dough onto each cookie sheet. Push and stretch them into round, flat shapes with your hands.

Arrange the toppings evenly over the tomato mixture, then sprinkle the grated cheese on top.

When the dough has risen, **knead** it for five minutes. Cut it into four equal pieces and shape them into balls.

Spread the tomato mixture over the pizzas with a wooden spoon. Don't spread it all the way to the edges.

They are ready when the edges are brown and crisp. TURN IT OFF

Cook for 20 minutes. Give one sheet ten minutes on the top shelf, then swap it with the one on the middle shelf.

Making a green salad

To prepare a head of lettuce, take off any broken leaves. Break off the rest of the leaves. Wash them in a colander.

Use cold water to wash the lettuce.

Hold the leaves down and shake them dry. Put them into a large bowl and shred them with your fingers.

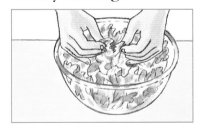

Peel and **chop** the cucumber into pieces. Wash the celery sticks. Chop off the ends, then slice them into little pieces.

Add to the lettuce and mix.

More about baking

To make some kinds of cakes or cookies, such as oatmeal bars, you melt some of the ingredients together in a saucepan before putting them into the oven. This is called the 'melting method' of baking. When you have made them you can decorate them with all sorts of things. Here you can see some ideas for decorations, but you could try using other ones.

Oatmeal bars

You will need:
2½ cups old-fashioned oats
½ cup packed brown sugar
¾ cup margarine
1 egg
3 tbs flour

7 x 11in cookie sheet,
paper towels,
medium-sized saucepan,
    wooden spoon, oven mitts,
    rounded knife, wire rack

For decorating the oatmeal bars you will need:
    4oz baking chocolate decorations such as candied cherries or pieces of candy

    small heat-proof bowl, small saucepan, wooden spoon, oven mitts, teaspoon

GET HELP

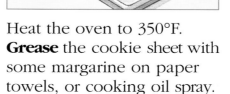

Heat the oven to 350°F. **Grease** the cookie sheet with some margarine on paper towels, or cooking oil spray.

HOT

Turn on a burner to low heat. Put the sugar and margarine into the larger saucepan.

Melting chocolate

Break the chocolate into pieces. Put it into a small bowl. Turn on a burner to low heat.

Half-fill a small saucepan with water and stand the bowl in it. Heat the water, but don't let it boil.

Stir with a wooden spoon.

When the chocolate has melted, lift the bowl out carefully. Use right away (see below).

Wear oven mitts.

Melt the mixture gently, stirring with a wooden spoon. When melted, take the pan off the heat.

Stir in the oats, egg and flour. Spoon the mixture onto the cookie sheet. Flatten it with the back of the spoon.

Bake on the middle shelf of the oven for 20-25 minutes. The oatmeal bars should be golden brown when cooked.

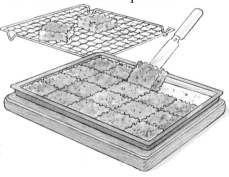

Cut into squares with a rounded knife. Allow to cool for 10-15 minutes, then take them out of the pan.

Decorating cakes and cookies

Scoop up some melted chocolate with a teaspoon. Let it drip over the cakes. Melt the chocolate again if it begins to go hard.

Make patterns, or smooth the chocolate with the spoon.

You can add decorations such as candied cherries or chocolate drops. Press them into the chocolate while it is still soft.

You could decorate brownies (see pages 10-11).

Making sauces

You can make delicious dishes out of simple things like pasta by adding a sauce to them. There are many different kinds of sauces. Here you can find out how to make white sauce, which is made with milk, flour and butter. In this recipe you then add cheese to make it into a cheese sauce, which is really tasty.

Tuna bake

You will need:
12oz cheese (3 cups grated)
6⅛ oz can tuna
7oz can sweet corn
3 cups pasta
   (elbow macaroni or
   any other pasta
   shape)
salt and pepper
a tomato and some
   fresh parsley

To make white sauce you will need:
6 tbs margarine
   or butter
6 tbs plain flour
3 cups milk

grater, plate, can opener, big saucepan, colander, medium saucepan, wooden spoon, measuring cup, whisk, oven-proof dish, oven mitts, kitchen knife, chopping board

To decorate the bake, arrange slices of tomato and little pieces of parsley on top before serving.

Grate the cheese. Open the cans of sweet corn and tuna and drain them into the sink.

Cook the pasta in a big saucepan for ten minutes. When cooked, drain with a strainer or a colander.

Make a white sauce in a medium saucepan (see right). When it thickens, take it off the heat.

Stir 2 cups of the cheese into the sauce. Add the sweet corn, tuna, and a pinch of salt and pepper.

Stir the mixture well, then pour it all into the big saucepan with the pasta. Mix everything together.

Making white sauce

Turn a burner or ring to medium heat. Melt the margarine gently.

Keep stirring in the milk a little at a time until it is all mixed in.

It will be a runny mixture.

Add the flour. Stir for one minute with a wooden spoon. Take off the heat.

Put the saucepan back on the heat. Heat up the sauce, stirring all the time.

Add a little of the milk. Stir well, then add a little more and mix it in.

As it heats up, the sauce will thicken. **Simmer** and stir for one minute.

Beat out any lumps with a whisk.

Spoon the mixture into an oven-proof dish. Scatter the rest of the cheese over the top.

Take the broiler pan from under the broiler to make more space. Turn the broiler on to full heat.

Put the dish under the broiler for about ten minutes, or until the cheese is golden brown and bubbling.

Cheesy pasta

Follow the steps for tuna bake, but use 3½ cups of cheese. Leave out the tuna. Leave in the sweet corn if you want to.

Cooking skills

This page explains some of the cooking skills and words that appear in this book and tells you a little bit more about them.

Beating - mixing something quickly and firmly with a wooden spoon or electric mixer.

Boiling - when a liquid or runny mixture is heated so that it becomes very hot and bubbles a lot.

Browning - cooking red meat, like beef, in hot oil until it turns brown all over.

Chopping - cutting something into chunks with a kitchen knife.

Cracking an egg - tapping the egg sharply on the edge of a cup or small bowl, putting your thumbs into the gap you have made and pulling the eggshell apart.

Creaming - beating margarine or butter and sugar together so that they become light and creamy.

Folding in - mixing one ingredient into another very gently with a metal spoon or rounded knife.

Grating - scraping a piece of food down the holes on a grater to make it into small pieces.

Kneading - pulling, pushing and folding dough so that it becomes smooth and stretchy.

Peeling - taking off the skin of a vegetable or fruit by cutting into it with a vegetable peeler, then scraping towards you.

Rolling out - making dough or pastry into a flat shape with a rolling pin.

Rubbing in - mixing flour and butter or margarine together with a knife, then your fingertips, to make a crumbly mixture.

Sifting - getting rid of any lumps in something like flour by putting it into a sifter and shaking it over a bowl. You can also push it through a strainer with the back of a metal spoon.

Simmering - when a liquid or runny mixture is hot, but only bubbling a little bit.

Slicing - cutting something with a kitchen knife to make thin pieces.

Squeezing a lemon - getting the juice from a lemon by putting one half over the top of a citrus juicer and twisting it to the left and to the right.

Whisking - adding lots of air to something by turning it quickly with a hand whisk, rotary whisk or electric mixer.

First published in 1995 by Usborne Publishing Ltd, Usborne House, 83-85 Saffron Hill, London EC1N 8RT, England. Copyright © 1995 Usborne Publishing Ltd. All rights reserved. No part of this publication may be reproduced, stored in a retrieval system, or transmitted by any means, electronic, mechanical, photocopying, recording or otherwise, without the prior permission of the publisher. The name Usborne and the device ♛ are the Trade Marks of Usborne Publishing Ltd. AE. First published in America March 1996. Printed in Belgium.